GERMANY 2016 HUMAN RIGHTS REPORT

EXECUTIVE SUMMARY

Germany is a constitutional democracy. Citizens choose their representatives periodically in free and fair multiparty elections. The lower chamber of the federal parliament (Bundestag) elects the head of the federal government, the chancellor. The second legislative chamber, the Federal Council (Bundesrat), represents the 16 states at the federal level and is composed of members of the state governments. Observers considered the 2013 national elections for the Bundestag to have been free and fair.

Civilian authorities maintained effective control over security forces.

The country faced the task of integrating the approximately 890,000 asylum seekers, refugees, and migrants who arrived in 2015, as well as the additional 256,000 who arrived during the first nine months of the year. The influx of asylum seekers, refugees, and migrants stretched the country's infrastructure and resources. It also exacerbated tensions within society.

Right-wing extremism and xenophobia were the most significant human rights problems. Perpetrators attacked ethnic non-Germans on a number of occasions, including acts of arson against government-run housing for asylum seekers, refugees, and migrants. Anti-Semitic acts also took place. Authorities attributed these incidents to adherents of the extreme right, as well as to some Muslims.

There were a number of other human rights problems. Authorities continued to extend the incarceration of certain categories of offenders past the completion of their sentences, asserting the offenders were a continuing threat to society. The detention of rejected asylum seekers awaiting deportation could be protracted. The government limited the freedoms of speech, press, assembly, and association of neo-Nazi and other groups deemed extremist or as threats to the constitution. The law excludes asylum seekers, refugees, and migrants from safe countries of origin from benefitting from most integration measures, such as language courses and reduced employment restrictions. There were reports of discrimination at the federal and state levels against some religious minorities, notably Scientologists and Muslims. There were also reports of gender-based violence--including against asylum seekers, refugees, and migrants--and the trafficking of men, women, and children for sexual exploitation and labor. Societal violence and discrimination based on sexual orientation persisted, as did some societal discrimination against persons with HIV/AIDS.

The government took steps to prosecute and punish officials in the security services and elsewhere in government who were deemed to have committed abuses.

Section 1. Respect for the Integrity of the Person, Including Freedom from:

a. Arbitrary Deprivation of Life and other Unlawful or Politically Motivated Killings

There were no reports that the government or its agents committed arbitrary or unlawful killings.

On December 19, Anis Amri allegedly killed Polish truck driver Lukasz Robert Urban and drove Urban's truck at high speed through a Christmas market on Breitscheidplatz in Berlin. The apparent terrorist attack killed 12 persons and injured 56. Amri fled and was killed in a shootout with police in Milan, Italy, on December 23.

b. Disappearance

There were no reports of politically motivated disappearances.

c. Torture and Other Cruel, Inhuman, or Degrading Treatment or Punishment

The constitution prohibits such practices, and there were few reports that government officials employed them.

In the reports on its 2010 and 2013 visits to the country, the Council of Europe's Committee for the Prevention of Torture (CPT) criticized the use of voluntary surgical castration as a means of treatment of incarcerated sex offenders, stating that it was a mutilating, irreversible intervention whose application to incarcerated sex offenders "could be considered as amounting to degrading treatment." The CPT recommended that all relevant federal and state authorities take steps to put a definitive end to its use. In a letter dated May 13, authorities informed the CPT no surgical castrations were performed on incarcerated sex offenders from 2013 to 2015.

In June, two police officers from Essen were cleared of charges of excessive use of force stemming from an April operation against drug dealers.

Prison and Detention Center Conditions

Prison and detention center conditions generally met international standards.

<u>Physical Conditions</u>: On May 4, an 18-year-old inmate at the Wuppertal-Ronsdorf Correctional Facility killed a 20-year-old man after a card game. The perpetrator had a history of violence.

<u>Independent Monitoring</u>: The government permitted monitoring by independent nongovernmental observers. A delegation from the CPT visited the country in 2015. As of year's end, the CPT's report had not been released.

d. Arbitrary Arrest or Detention

The constitution prohibits arbitrary arrest and detention, and the government generally observed these prohibitions.

Role of the Police and Security Apparatus

Responsibility for internal and border security is shared by the police forces of the 16 states and the Federal Criminal Police Office (BKA) and the Federal Police. The states' police forces report to their respective interior ministries; the federal police forces report to the Federal Ministry of the Interior. The Federal Office for the Protection of the Constitution (FOPC) and the state offices for the protection of the constitution (OPCs) are responsible for gathering intelligence on threats to domestic order and certain other security functions. Like police, the OPCs report to their respective state ministries of the interior. Civilian authorities maintained effective control over police and the OPCs, and the government has effective mechanisms to investigate and punish abuse and corruption. There were no reports of impunity involving the security forces during the year. The nongovernmental organization (NGO) Amnesty International Germany stated that there is no nationwide requirement for police to wear identity badges. According to the NGO, police are required to wear badges in Berlin and Brandenburg, as are riot police in Rhineland-Palatinate, Hesse, Bremen, and Schleswig-Holstein.

In September 2015 Cologne's police chief dissolved the city's special forces unit and suspended 15 of its members while the city's prosecutor's office investigated abusive initiation practices and the misuse of a police helicopter to take private photographs. During the year the prosecutor's office closed these investigations due to a lack of evidence, and the new Cologne police chief allowed all the officers involved to return to their previous assignments.

Arrest Procedures and Treatment of Detainees

Authorities may arrest an individual only with a warrant issued by a competent judicial authority unless police apprehend a suspect in the act of committing a crime or have strong reason to believe that the individual intends to commit a crime. The constitution provides that authorities must produce an apprehended person before a judge no later than the day after the suspect was taken into custody. At that time the judge must inform the suspect of the reasons for the detention and provide the suspect an opportunity to object. The court must then either issue an arrest warrant stating the grounds for detention or order the individual's release. Authorities generally respected these rights.

Bail exists, but authorities granted it infrequently. Judges usually released individuals awaiting trial without requiring bail, except in cases where a court decided there was a clear risk that the individual might flee. In such cases authorities may hold detainees for the duration of the investigation and subsequent trial, subject to judicial review. Time spent in investigative custody applies toward any eventual sentence. If a court acquits an incarcerated defendant, the government must compensate the defendant for financial losses as well as for "moral prejudice" due to the incarceration.

The law entitles a detainee to prompt access to an attorney at any time, including prior to any police questioning. According to the law, before interrogations begin authorities must inform suspects, arrested or not, of their right to consult an attorney.

In December 2015 an administrative court in Cologne ruled illegal the involuntary strip-searches of detainees by police for contraband. This decision stemmed from a complaint from a woman arrested and involuntarily strip-searched in 2013.

The law does not allow courts to punish persons twice for the same crime. A court may, however, order an offender convicted of rape, homicide, or manslaughter to spend additional time in "subsequent preventive detention" after completing the offender's sentence, if it determines that the offender suffers from a mental disorder or represents a continuing serious danger to the public. The law permits the imposition of such detention for an indefinite period, subject to periodic reviews.

Because the law does not regard such detention as punishment, authorities are legally required to keep subsequent prevention detainees in separate buildings or in special prison sections with better conditions than those of the general prison population. Authorities must also provide a range of social and psychological therapy programs. According to the Federal Statistics Office, at the end of March 524 offenders, including one woman, were being held in subsequent preventive detention.

<u>Detainee's Ability to Challenge Lawfulness of Detention before Court</u>: A detainee has the right to appeal his or her detention at any point of the sentence. The regional court of appeal decides whether to grant the appeal. It must hear the detainee and other persons involved unless it is firmly convinced that this will lead to no new findings. If the court of appeal holds that detention is to be continued, the detainee has a further right to appeal to the Federal High Court.

<u>Protracted Detention of Rejected Asylum Seekers or Stateless Persons</u>: Authorities in various states continued the practice of detaining rejected asylum seekers awaiting deportation, sometimes for protracted periods.

In 2014 the Federal Court of Justice ruled that authorities may detain asylum seekers, refugees, and migrants awaiting deportation to a country within the EU under Dublin procedures only if there was evidence they might abscond. Court rulings required authorities to move unsuccessful asylum seekers awaiting deportation from prisons to separate, special facilities with less strict security measures. As of October 2015, only five states had separate facilities, although some states shared facilities. Authorities may return asylum seekers, refugees, and migrants who are from safe countries of origin or who are not eligible for asylum without giving prior notice.

e. Denial of Fair Public Trial

The constitution provides for an independent judiciary, and the government generally respected judicial independence.

Trial Procedures

The constitution provides for the right to a fair and public trial, and an independent judiciary generally enforced this right. Defendants enjoy a presumption of innocence and have the right to be informed promptly and in detail of the charges against them, with free interpretation as necessary. The trial shall be fair, public, and held without undue delay. The law requires that defendants be present at their trials. A single judge, a panel of professional judges, or a mixed panel of professional and nonprofessional judges may try a case, depending on the severity of the charges. Defendants have the right to consult with an attorney, and the government provides an attorney at public expense if defendants demonstrate financial need. Defendants and their attorneys have the right to adequate time and facilities to prepare a defense. They have access to all court-held evidence relevant to their cases. Defendants may confront and question adverse witnesses and present witnesses and evidence on their behalf. Defendants may not be compelled to testify or confess guilt. Defendants have a right of appeal. These rights extend to all citizens.

Political Prisoners and Detainees

There were no reports of political prisoners or detainees.

Civil Judicial Procedures and Remedies

Citizens may file complaints about violations of their human rights with petition committees and commissioners for citizens' affairs. Citizens usually referred to these points of contact as "ombudsmen." Additionally, an independent and impartial judiciary in civil matters provides court access for lawsuits seeking damages for, or cessation of, a human rights violation. Persons who exhaust domestic legal remedies may appeal cases involving alleged government violations of the European Convention on Human Rights to the European Court of Human Rights.

f. Arbitrary or Unlawful Interference with Privacy, Family, Home, or Correspondence

The constitution prohibits such actions, and there were no reports the government failed to respect these prohibitions.

The federal and state OPCs continued to monitor political groupings deemed potentially hostile to the constitution, including the Left Party and the right-wing extremist National Democratic Party (NPD). Authorities stated they employed monitoring as a last resort but only with approval of state or federal interior ministries and review by state or federal parliamentary intelligence committees. Authorities indicated they monitored the Left Party, which had seats in the Bundestag, because of their perception that it tolerated left-extremist groups within its ranks.

All OPC activities are challengeable in court, including ultimately in the Federal Constitutional Court. In 2014 following a Constitutional Court ruling, the government indicated that the FOPC would no longer observe Bundestag members.

In an August 30 report, the UN special rapporteur for privacy noted that "the democratic oversight of intelligence services in the country remains a cause for concern." Echoing the concerns of the commissioner for human rights of the Council of Europe in his report in October 2015, the special rapporteur noted that the oversight bodies in the country lacked resources and technical expertise. He also stated there is no judicial review over the agencies' activities.

Section 2. Respect for Civil Liberties, Including:

a. Freedom of Speech and Press

The constitution provides for freedom of speech and press, and the government generally respected these rights. An independent press, an effective judiciary, and a functioning democratic political system combined to promote freedom of speech and press. The law bans Nazi propaganda, Holocaust denial, and fomenting racial hatred.

Freedom of Speech and Expression: While the government generally respected these rights, it imposed limits on groups it deemed extremist. The government arrested, tried, convicted, and imprisoned a number of individuals for speech that incited racial hatred, endorsed Nazism, or denied the Holocaust (see also section 6, Anti-Semitism).

In April a Cologne local court fined a 39-year-old man 2,250 euros ($2,480) for performing the Hitler salute and shouting repeatedly "Heil Hitler" and "Sieg Heil" in February 2015. The man stated that he regretted his actions, explaining that he was drunk and surrounded by right-wing extremists at the time. After the incident, the accused participated in an exit program for right-wing radicals and underwent treatment for alcoholism.

On November 7, a Brandenburg state court convicted and sentenced a member of the NPD to eight months in prison for displaying a Nazi-style tattoo that appeared to combine an image of the Auschwitz death camp with the slogan from the Buchenwald concentration camp's gate, "Jedem das Seine"--"To each his own."

Press and Media Freedoms: On October 21, the Bundestag approved amendments to the law regulating the country's foreign intelligence service, the BND. Proponents argued that the amendments increased oversight, and enhanced the protection of the rights of German and EU citizens and institutions. The NGOs Reporters without Borders and Amnesty International expressed concern that the law would allow surveillance of foreign journalists abroad. A government spokesperson stated that the new law is consistent with freedom of the press. There were no known reports of either surveillance of journalists or any other allegations of actual abuses as a result of the amendments.

Violence and Harassment: In March the NGO Committee to Protect Journalists reported journalists' access to camps for asylum seekers, refugees, and migrants, varied depending on the state. Activists of the extreme right-wing anti-Muslim campaign group Patriotic Europeans Against the Islamization of the West (PEGIDA) booed and physically attacked journalists reporting on their rallies.

Censorship or Content Restrictions: On March 31, comedian Jan Boehmermann read on national state-funded ZDF-TV a deliberately offensive poem about Turkish President Recep Tayyip Erdogan containing profanity and allegations regarding President Erdogan's sexual practices. In response the Turkish government requested that the German government prosecute Boehmermann for defamation of a head of state under Sections 103 and 104 of the country's criminal code. The government referred the case to the state prosecutor in Mainz, who dropped the case in October after determining that there was insufficient evidence that a criminal act occurred. Also in October the Public Prosecutor's Office in Koblenz rejected President Erdogan's appeal to resume the trial. A decision is expected in February 2017 on a separate civil case filed by President Erdogan regarding the incident.

Internet Freedom

The government did not restrict or disrupt access to the internet or censor online content, and there were no credible reports that the government monitored private online communications without appropriate legal authority. The law allows the government to take down websites that belong to banned organizations or include speech that incites racial hatred, endorses Nazism, or denies the Holocaust. Authorities worked directly with internet service providers and online media companies to monitor and in some cases remove such content.

On November 4, prosecutors in Munich confirmed that they were investigating Mark Zuckerberg and nine other Facebook executives, including Chief Operating Officer Sheryl Sandberg. A Bavarian lawyer filed a complaint in September, alleging that the company broke national laws against hate speech and sedition by failing to remove racist postings. The lawyer has compiled a list of 438 postings that were flagged as inappropriate but not deleted, including racist hate speech, calls to violence, and references to Nazi-era genocide. Prosecutors are obliged by law to investigate complaints. A decision to prosecute or dismiss was not yet reached in the Munich investigation by year's end. This filing followed a similar complaint by the same lawyer in Hamburg. The Public Prosecutor in Hamburg dismissed that case early in the year.

On April 4, Berlin police searched the apartments of 10 persons who had posted statements that supported shooting asylum seekers, refugees, and migrants at the borders and included anti-Semitic views. On July 13, the BKA coordinated a nationwide raid in 14 states.

According to the International Telecommunication Union, in 2015, 88 percent of the country's population used the internet, and 37 percent had a fixed broadband subscription.

As of July the taskforce of North Rhine-Westphalia (NRW) to combat cybercrime had begun 192 investigations into right-wing online harassment.

In June a Duesseldorf court sentenced a 14-year-old high school student from Duesseldorf to 20 hours of community service, after she secretly photographed her teacher in class and uploaded the picture with a defamatory caption to a website with a relatively large viewership.

Academic Freedom and Cultural Events

There were some government restrictions on academic freedom and cultural events supporting extreme right-wing neo-Nazism.

b. Freedom of Peaceful Assembly and Association

Freedom of Assembly

The constitution and law provide for freedom of assembly, and the government generally respected this right. Groups seeking to hold open-air public rallies and marches must obtain permits, and state and local officials may deny permits when public safety concerns arise or when the applicant is from a prohibited organization, mainly right-wing extremist groups. In rare instances during the year, authorities denied such applications to assemble publicly. Authorities allowed several nonprohibited, right-wing extremist or neo-Nazi groups to hold public rallies or marches when they did so in accordance with the law.

It is illegal to block an officially registered demonstration, including demonstrations organized by neo-Nazi groups. Many anti-Nazi activists refused to accept such restrictions and attempted to block neo-Nazi demonstrations or to hold counterdemonstrations, resulting in clashes between police and anti-Nazi demonstrators.

Police detained known or suspected activists, primarily right- or left-wing extremists, when they believed such individuals intended to participate in illegal or unauthorized demonstrations. The length of detention varied from state to state.

Freedom of Association

The constitution provides for freedom of association, and the government generally respected this right. The law permits authorities to prohibit organizations whose activities the Constitutional Court or federal or state governments determine to be opposed to the constitutional democratic order or otherwise illegal. While only the Federal Constitutional Court may prohibit political parties on these grounds, both federal and state governments may prohibit or restrict other organizations, including groups that authorities classify as extremist or criminal in nature. Organizations have the right to appeal such prohibitions or restrictions.

The federal and state OPCs monitored several hundred organizations. Monitoring generally consisted of collecting information from written materials and firsthand accounts but also included intrusive methods, such as the use of undercover agents who were subject to legal oversight. The FOPC and state OPCs published lists of monitored organizations, including left- and right-wing political parties. Although the law stipulates that surveillance must not interfere with an organization's activities, representatives of monitored groups, such as Scientologists, complained that the publication of the organizations' names contributed to prejudice against them. In a number of cases, authorities banned organizations and raided their premises. Authorities stated that they took such actions if there was evidence the groups or persons were incompatible with--or caused a threat to--the country's democratic order.

On March 16, Interior Minister Thomas de Maiziere banned the right-wing extremist group Weisse Woelfe Terrorcrew (WWT) following searches of WWT leaders' apartments in 10 states. De Maiziere stated in a press release that during these raids officials found propaganda material and weapons, including throwing stars, a crossbow, and several small-caliber firearms. The Hamburg-based WWT consisted of neo-Nazis and former skinheads who committed violence against immigrants, asylum seekers, refugees, and migrants, as well as the police. According to the *Report on Protection of the Constitution*, the WWT was active nationwide beginning in 2014.

c. Freedom of Religion

See the Department of State's *International Religious Freedom Report* at www.state.gov/religiousfreedomreport/.

d. Freedom of Movement, Internally Displaced Persons, Protection of Refugees, and Stateless Persons

The constitution provides for freedom of internal movement, foreign travel, emigration, and repatriation; the government generally respected these rights.

Abuse of Migrants, Refugees, and Stateless Persons: The NGO Pro Asyl, which tracks cases of refugees, criticized the "fast procedure" for asylum seekers, refugees, and migrants who arrive at the country's airports. The procedure provides for the Federal Office for Migration and Refugees to decide on asylum applications within an expedited two-day period during which time it detains applicants at the airport. If authorities deny the application, the applicant may appeal the ruling. Authorities make a final decision on the appeal within two weeks, during which time the applicant remains in detention at the airport. If authorities deny the appeal, they subsequently deport the applicant. Authorities maintained that they applied this fast procedure only to persons coming from safe countries of origin and to persons without valid identification documents. Pro Asyl stated that the number of asylum seekers rejected under the fast procedure was relatively low at 300-500 cases annually and that the vast majority of asylum seekers entered the country before they filed their applications. Pro Asyl cited the case of an Afghan refugee who was initially denied asylum via the fast procedure at the airport. The case went to the Constitutional Court, which overruled the asylum rejection.

Instances of assault on refugees, asylum seekers, refugees, and migrants and attacks on government-provided asylum homes--including incidents of arson and hate-speech graffiti--remained at a high level during the first half of the year. According to BKA's figures, from January to October authorities registered 832 offenses committed at refugee and asylum shelters or directly aimed at the shelters. The total number included 144 violent offenses (compared with 28 in 2014).

According to the Baden-Wuerttemberg Ministry of Interior, the number of attacks against asylum seekers', refugees', and migrants' homes in Baden-Wuerttemberg increased during the year compared with 2015. In 2015, nine attacks against refugee housing sites in the state were reported, compared with 13 incidents as of July 1. In the early morning hours of August 31, unknown perpetrators set on fire a refugee shelter in Weil am Rhein (southern Baden-Wuerttemberg). The shelter was previously attacked in October 2015.

On February 9, in Escheburg in the state of Schleswig-Holstein, a man firebombed a center for asylum seekers, refugees, and migrants. In May he was convicted and sentenced to two years in prison.

On September 29, a storage building burned down in Oberteuringen, Baden-Wurttemberg in what the police suspected to be arson. The building was to house up to 70 asylum seekers, refugees, and migrants.

On June 19, in Volkmarsen, Hesse, a housing container in which authorities planned to house asylum seekers, refugees, and migrants was set on fire. In addition 29 swastikas were spray painted on the container.

The government cooperated with the Office of the UN High Commissioner for Refugees (UNHCR) and other humanitarian organizations in providing protection and assistance to internally displaced persons, refugees, returning refugees, asylum seekers, stateless persons, or other persons of concern.

Protection of Refugees

Access to Asylum: Laws provide for the granting of asylum or refugee status, and the government has established a system for providing protection to refugees. In the first six months of the year, 222,264 asylum seekers, refugees, and migrants arrived in the country. Federal, state, and local authorities registered almost all new arrivals under existing laws and regulations.

Safe Country of Origin/Transit: The country adheres to the EU's Dublin III regulation, which permits authorities to turn back or deport individuals who entered the country through a "safe country of transit."

The Federal Interior Ministry continued its policy of excluding Greece as a safe country to which it could return asylum seekers, refugees, and migrants, citing systemic failures in Greece's asylum system.

Refoulement: There were reports that authorities deported Roma and others to countries of the Balkans, including Kosovo. In May in Berlin, 200 Roma protested their possible deportations.

Employment: Under an integration law passed in August, if a refugee or asylum seeker who is not from a "safe country of origin" starts vocational training, the term of his or her residence permit will correspond to the training period. If the refugee or asylum seeker finishes the training successfully, the residence permit may be extended by up to six months to look for a job, and by two years if they receive a job offer. Refugees and asylum seekers may work in any sector and are eligible for subcontracted work via temporary work agencies. Other hurdles to employment remained, such as long review times for recognition of previous qualifications and a lack of language skills and official certificates. This law does not apply to asylum seekers, refugees, and migrants from safe countries of origin.

Access to Basic Services: NGOs and civil society organizations in all states provided additional support for new arrivals, including accommodation, meals, transportation, childcare, and medical and psychological care. Because standard apartment or dormitory housing was insufficient for the number of asylum seekers, refugees, and migrants arriving in 2015 and 2016, state and local officials housed large groups of them--often on cots--in temporary emergency accommodations across the country, including gymnasiums, indoor stadiums, former schools and office complexes, large tents, and container-sized shelters. Most of these emergency shelters were emptied, and asylum seekers, refugees, and migrants were housed again in dormitories or apartments. The decision on how to house asylum seekers, refugees, and migrants and whether to provide cash benefits or other contributions is up to local officials in each state. For example, the state of Berlin continued to operate emergency shelters, among them at the former Tempelhof Airport and in gymnasiums.

Asylum seekers and those with a successfully finished asylum process that have a job or vocational training offer are permitted to change their assigned place of residence.

The NGO Aerzte der Welt criticized medical care for asylum seekers, which was in most cases only free of charge when the patient suffered from acute illness or pain. A few states provided medical insurance cards. Some local communities and private groups initiated additional health-care projects. The head of a Berlin refugee shelter said that, especially for asylum seekers, refugees and migrants needing psychological treatments, the lack of interpreters was a pressing concern. She recounted one case in which a woman was in a closed psychiatric facility for four months before she had access to an interpreter and was able to explain her case to the doctors.

Federal, state, and civil society efforts contributed to the promulgation of information for asylum seekers, refugees, and migrants in Arabic, Urdu, Farsi, and other languages about basic rights and customs in the country.

Durable Solutions: The government accepted for resettlement refugees who had already fled their countries of origin and facilitated local integration (including naturalization), particularly for refugees belonging to vulnerable groups. Such groups included women with children, refugees with disabilities, and victims of torture or rape. The government assisted with the safe and voluntary return of migrants, asylum seekers, refugees, and migrants to their homes. Authorities granted residence permits to long-term migrants, asylum seekers, refugees, and migrants with no prospects of returning to their home countries.

Temporary Protection: The government also provided protection to individuals who did not qualify as refugees. In the first six months of the year, the government extended subsidiary protection to 23,302 persons and humanitarian protection to an estimated 2,120 others.

Stateless Persons

UNHCR reported 12,969 stateless persons in the country at the end of 2015. Some of these persons lost their previous citizenship when the Soviet Union collapsed or Yugoslavia disintegrated. Others were Palestinians from Lebanon and Syria who were registered as stateless in the country.

The government generally implemented laws and policies to provide stateless persons the opportunity to gain citizenship on a nondiscriminatory basis. Stateless persons may apply for citizenship after six years of residence, but producing sufficient evidence to establish statelessness could be difficult, since the burden of proof is on the applicant. Authorities generally protected stateless persons from deportation to their country of origin or usual residence if they faced a threat of political persecution there.

Section 3. Freedom to Participate in the Political Process

The constitution provides citizens the ability to choose their government in free and fair periodic elections held by secret ballot and based on universal and equal suffrage.

Elections and Political Participation

Recent Elections: Observers considered the parliamentary elections in 2013 free and fair.

Political Parties and Political Participation: Political parties generally operated without restriction or outside interference unless authorities deemed them a threat to the federal constitution. When federal authorities perceive such a threat, they may petition the Federal Constitutional Court to ban the party. The court banned two parties in the 1950s.

On June 10, the NRW state parliament amended the state constitution to require that parties meet a 2.5 percent threshold of the total vote to enter local governments. The basis for this change was concern regarding the increasing number of fragmented local governments that found it difficult to find compromise positions. On July 29, the state chapter of the right-wing extremist NPD challenged the amendment in court, arguing it violated the party's right to equality in elections. At year's end the case was pending with the NRW Constitutional Court in Muenster.

<u>Participation of Women and Minorities</u>: No laws limit the participation of women and members of minorities in the political process, and they participated.

Section 4. Corruption and Lack of Transparency in Government

The law provides criminal penalties for corruption by officials, and the government generally implemented the law effectively.

In February a local court in Bonn dismissed a claim for nonpayment after a member of the local Pro NRW right-wing party did not receive payment from a fellow party member to whom he had sold his Bonn city council seat in 2014. In dismissing the case, the court ruled that one cannot sell a legitimate democratic mandate.

<u>Corruption</u>: The Brandenburg state prosecutor's office investigated a case of corruption. On October 17, a former procurement official of the airport management company of the Berlin-Brandenburg airport was sentenced to three years in prison for corruption related to the airport's construction.

<u>Financial Disclosure</u>: Members of state and federal parliaments are subject to financial disclosure laws that require them to publish their earnings from outside employment. They must disclose earnings from outside regular employment that are greater than 1,000 euros ($1,100) in a month in 10 different income categories, with the highest category being for income above 250,000 euros ($275,000) per month. Disclosures are available to the public via the Bundestag's website and in the *Official Handbook of the Bundestag*. Sanctions for noncompliance range from an administrative fine to as much as half of a parliamentarian's annual salary. Appointed officials are subject to the public disclosure rules for civil servants, who must disclose outside activity and earnings. If the remuneration exceeds certain limits, which vary by grade, the civil servant must transfer the excess to the employing agency.

<u>Public Access to Information</u>: Federal law provides for public access to government information, but there are numerous exceptions. Fees for record searches could be as much as 500 euros ($550), payable in advance. Of the 16 states, 12 also have freedom-of-information laws. There is an appeals process.

Section 5. Governmental Attitude Regarding International and Nongovernmental Investigation of Alleged Violations of Human Rights

Domestic and international human rights groups operated without government restriction, investigating and publishing their findings on human rights cases. Government officials were cooperative and responsive to their views.

Government Human Rights Bodies: A wide range of government bodies and NGOs worked to protect human rights. The Bundestag has a Committee for Human Rights and Humanitarian Aid as well as a Petitions Committee. The latter fields a variety of complaints from the public, including human rights concerns. The German Institute for Human Rights has responsibility for monitoring the country's implementation of its international human rights commitments, including human rights treaties and conventions. The Federal Antidiscrimination Agency (FADA) is a semi-independent body that studies discrimination and supports victims of discrimination. The Office of the Federal Commissioner for Persons with Disabilities has specific responsibility for protecting the rights of persons with disabilities. A commissioner of human rights within the Justice Ministry oversees implementation of decisions by the courts, whose rulings continue to refine human rights protections.

Section 6. Discrimination, Societal Abuses, and Trafficking in Persons

Women

Rape and Domestic Violence: The law criminalizes rape, including spousal rape, and provides penalties of up to 15 years in prison.

On July 7, the Bundestag passed a law that implemented a "no means no" rule: If the nonconsent of the victim is apparent and the perpetrator overrides this will, the act is defined as rape. The Bundestag also approved a change of the criminal code to include a provision on offenses committed by groups. Possible penalties are a fine or up to two-years' imprisonment.

Officials may temporarily deny abusers access to the household without a court order, put them under a restraining order, or in severe cases prosecute them for assault or rape and require them to pay damages. Penalties depend on the nature of the case. The government enforced the law.

The government devoted considerable personnel and financial resources to the problem. Approximately 12,000 to 13,000 cases of sexual violence are reported annually to the police. According to the Federal Office for Family and Civic

Tasks, approximately every fourth woman between ages 16 and 85 has been a victim of domestic violence at least once in her life.

According to the Federal Criminal Police Office, 127,457 persons in relationships were targets of murder, bodily harm, rape, sexual assault, threats and stalking in 2015. Approximately 82 percent--or more than 104,000--of these were women.

The federal government, the states, and NGOs supported numerous projects to deal with gender-based violence, both to prevent it and to give victims greater access to medical care and legal assistance.

During the year approximately 350 women's shelters operated. According to the NGO Central Information Agency of Autonomous Women's Homes (ZIF), an estimated 18,000 women, plus their children, used the shelters annually. ZIF reported accessibility problems, especially in bigger cities, as women who found refuge in a shelter tended to stay there longer than needed because they could not find an apartment due to a lack of available and affordable housing. No statistics indicated refugee women contributed to this shortage of available spaces, but ZIF stated the number of refugee women seeking protection in shelters rose since the fall of 2015. Since asylum seekers, refugees, and migrants are not eligible for social welfare benefits while their applications for asylum are under review, cost is another obstacle refugee women face in finding a place to live in a shelter.

The national 24-hour hotline of the Federal Office for Family and Civic Tasks had a staff of 60 persons who provided counseling to affected women in 15 languages. In 2015 the hotline was contacted 55,000 times and provided 27,000 counseling sessions. Many NGOs at the local level also provided hotlines, assistance, advice, and shelter.

During the year the NRW state government approved the continuation of 900,000 euros ($990,000) in funding to provide counseling and support for traumatized refugee survivors of violence. Implementation of the program is in cooperation with regional associations.

Female Genital Mutilation/Cutting (FGM/C): FGM/C of women and girls is a criminal offense punishable by one to 15 years in prison. FGM/C affected segments of the immigrant population and their German-born children, but official statistics were limited.

<u>Other Harmful Traditional Practices</u>: Forced marriages are illegal, invalid, and punishable by up to five-years' imprisonment. There were no reliable statistics on the number of forced marriages. Papatya, a Berlin-based NGO that supports migrant and post-migrant female victims of domestic violence or forced marriage, stated that the problem was more prevalent in the Muslim and Yazidi communities than in the general population. Forced marriages reportedly often led to violence. Victims included women and in some cases men whose families arranged for them to acquire spouses from abroad. Some families also sent women to other countries to marry against their will.

A representative from Papatya recounted cases where the Ministry of Foreign Affairs helped victims of forced marriage to return to the country. Some cases included girls who held dual citizenship in Germany and the country to which they were sent for a forced marriage. In these cases German authorities have no power to return victims to Germany from a country in which the victim holds citizenship.

The law criminalizes "honor killings" as murder and provides penalties that include life in prison. The government enforced the law effectively.

In June the court proceedings regarding the death of 35-year-old Hanaa S. began in Wuppertal, NRW. Authorities believed the Iraqi-Yazidi was the victim of an honor killing carried out by five of her relatives after she left her husband in 2014 and moved in with another man.

<u>Sexual Harassment</u>: Sexual harassment of women was a recognized problem. It is prohibited by law. On June 7, the Bundestag approved a change of the criminal code to include a provision on sexual harassment. The law requires employers to protect employees from sexual harassment. Various disciplinary measures against harassment in the workplace were available, including dismissal of the perpetrator. The law considers an employer's failure to take measures to protect employees from sexual harassment to be a breach of contract, and an affected employee has the right to paid leave until the employer rectifies the problem. According to a 2015 study conducted by the Federal Anti-Discrimination Agency, more than 50 percent of all employees either experienced or witnessed sexual harassment at work. Of the sample, 81 percent were unaware of the employer's duty to protect them proactively from sexual harassment at work, and more than 70 percent did not know a contact person for this problem in their company. Unions, churches, government agencies, and NGOs operated a variety of support programs for women who experienced sexual harassment and sponsored seminars and training to prevent it.

On New Year's Eve, December 31, 2015, widespread assaults on women caused a public outcry. The attacks occurred primarily in Cologne but also happened in other NRW cities such as Duesseldorf, Dortmund, and Bielefeld. According to the NRW Interior Ministry, as of March 30, there were reports of 1,200 separate criminal acts in Cologne alone. As of October 7, the Cologne local court concluded 19 trials related to the attacks. It convicted 20 defendants of theft, one for sexual assault, and one for sexual insult. Of these 22 suspects, 10 held Algerian citizenship, nine Moroccan, one Iraqi, one Libyan, and one Tunisian. Sentences ranged from a 480-euro ($528) fine to 20 months in prison. In February the NRW state parliament formed a special investigatory committee regarding the attacks which continued at year's end.

In Hamburg more than 300 women reported being sexually harassed or assaulted while celebrating New Year's Eve 2015. On January 14, police announced that, of 195 complaints received, they had identified eight suspects. In at least one case, authorities initiated legal proceedings against a suspect, but concluded no successful prosecutions by year's end.

In response the Bundestag also changed the criminal code to include a provision on sexual harassment and on offenses committed by groups. Committing such an offense could potentially affect a noncitizen's chances of obtaining a residence permit.

Reproductive Rights: Couples and individuals have the right to decide the number, spacing, and timing of their children; manage their reproductive health; and have access to the information and means to do so, free from discrimination, coercion, or violence.

Discrimination: Men and women enjoy the same legal status and rights under the constitution, including in family, labor, religious, personal status, property, nationality, and inheritance laws. The law provides for equal pay for equal work. Women were underrepresented in highly paid managerial positions and overrepresented in some lower-wage occupations (see section 7.d.).

In July a fourth woman was appointed judge to the second of two chambers of the Federal Constitutional Court that now has a 50-50 male-female ratio. The first chamber consisted of six men and two women.

Children

<u>Birth Registration</u>: In most cases persons derive citizenship from their parents, but the law also allows citizenship based on birth in the country if one parent has been a resident for at least eight years or has had a permanent residence permit for at least three years. Parents or guardians have the responsibility to apply for registration for newborn children. Once officials receive registration applications, they generally process them expeditiously. Parents who fail to register their child's birth may be subject to a fine.

<u>Child Abuse</u>: There were reported incidents of child abuse. The Federal Ministry for Family, Seniors, Women, and Youth sponsored a number of programs throughout the year on the prevention of child abuse. The ministry sought to create networks among parents, youth services, schools, pediatricians, and courts and to support existing programs at the state and local level. Other programs provided therapy and support for adult and youth victims of sexual abuse. The Early Help program created and expanded networks to support first-time parents facing social and economic challenges. In May the federal government installed an independent commission consisting of seven members to look into cases of child abuse. Both the Roman Catholic and Protestant churches announced their cooperation with the commission.

<u>Early and Forced Marriage</u>: The legal minimum age for marriage is 18. Forced marriages are invalid and illegal and are punishable by a prison sentence of up to five years. According to BKA statistics, there were 50 reported forced marriages; however, many cases went unreported and unrecorded.

Child and forced marriage affected mostly girls. The media reported that more than 1,400 cases of child marriage were registered with authorities and that more than 1,100 were girls. Nearly half of the cases reported involved nationals from Syria; other countries of origin were Iraq, Bulgaria, Poland, Romania, and Greece. State authorities considered these girls unaccompanied minors who are required to enter the care of the Child Welfare Office and to be separated from their husbands. Some NGOs criticized this practice as not necessarily supportive of the women concerned, arguing that an individual examination of cases would be more effective than the application of a standard procedure.

The Higher Regional Court in Bamberg, Bavaria, accepted the marriage between a 15-year old Syrian girl and her 21-year-old cousin because it found no signs of forced marriage in this specific case, and ruled that the girl herself should be able to decide on her contact with her husband.

<u>Female Genital Mutilation/Cutting (FGM/C)</u>: See information for girls younger than 18 in the section on women above.

<u>Sexual Exploitation of Children</u>: The penalty for rape--up to 15 years in prison--also applies to the rape of children. Consensual sex is legal from age 14 in most cases. There is an exception if the older partner is older than 18 and is "exploiting a coercive situation" or offering compensation and the younger partner is under 16. It is also illegal for a person age 21 or older to have sex with a child under age 16 if the older person "exploits the victim's lack of capacity for sexual self-determination." In 2015 according to the BKA, almost 14,000 cases of sexual abuse against children were reported. The BKA stated that many cases were unreported. The government's Independent Commissioner for Child Sex Abuse Issues offered a sexual abuse help online portal and an anonymous helpline on sexual abuse that was free of charge.

Possession of or attempts to acquire any material reflecting a true or realistic incident of child pornography is punishable by imprisonment from three months to five years. According to criminal statistics published by the BKA, in 2015 there were 6,560 cases involving the distribution of child pornography, and ownership and procurement of child pornography.

<u>Displaced Children</u>: There were no reliable statistics on the number of street children. Some observers indicated that there were several thousand, but authorities contended that such estimates were inflated and not a true representation of the often temporary status of homeless children. Authorities believed these children were frequently fleeing violent and abusive homes. Street children often turned to prostitution for income.

As of July the media reported that around 9,000 unaccompanied minor asylum seekers, refugees, and migrants were not accounted for. According to the Interior Ministry and the NGO Federal Association for Unaccompanied Minor Refugees (BumF), many of these minors moved on to relatives in the country and abroad. BumF stated that some unaccompanied minors may have become victims of human trafficking.

According to the year's estimates by Off Road Kids, an NGO active nationwide in street social work in major cities, there were up to 2,500 runaways per year under age 18. Of these, more than 300 ended up living on the streets.

<u>International Child Abductions</u>: The country is a party to the 1980 Hague Convention on the Civil Aspects of International Child Abduction. See the Department of State's *Annual Report on International Parental Child Abduction* at travel.state.gov/content/childabduction/en/legal/compliance.html.

Anti-Semitism

Observers estimated the country's Jewish population to be almost 250,000, of whom an estimated 90 percent were from the former Soviet Union. There were 110,000 registered Jewish community members. Manifestations of anti-Semitism, including physical and verbal attacks, occurred at public demonstrations, sporting and social events, and in certain media. Apart from anti-Semitic speech, desecration of cemeteries and Holocaust monuments represented the most widespread anti-Semitic acts. The federal government attributed most anti-Semitic acts to neo-Nazi or other right-wing extremist groups or persons. Jewish organizations also noted an increase of anti-Semitic attitudes among some Muslim youth.

The FOPC's annual report stated that the number of right-wing and violent anti-Semitic incidents declined from 31 in 2014 to 29 in 2015. On International Holocaust Remembrance Day, January 27, unknown perpetrators knocked down six gravestones in a Jewish cemetery in the town of Kropelin, near Rostock. On about February 2, vandals in Berlin defaced with gray paint "stumbling block" memorials, small brass blocks set into sidewalks marking the last home of Jewish victims of the Holocaust.

The FOPC noted that membership in skinhead and neo-Nazi groups remained steady at approximately 6,000 persons. Federal prosecutors brought charges against suspects and maintained permanent security measures around many synagogues.

In February a local appeals court affirmed that the action of two men who threw Molotov cocktails at the main synagogue in Wuppertal was "anti-Israeli" and not "anti-Semitic." Nevertheless, the unsuccessful appeal led to an increase in the probationary sentences to two years and one year and 11 months for the two attackers.

On February 7, Peter Schmalenbach, a board member of the right-wing populist Alternative for Germany (AfD) party and a resident of Neuwied in the state of

Rhineland-Palatinate, posted anti-Semitic slogans on his Facebook page. He removed the Facebook post shortly thereafter.

On July 5, the AfD caucus in the Baden-Wuerttemberg state parliament split into two caucuses after AfD Deputy Wolfgang Gedeon refused to dissociate himself from his anti-Semitic publications. Gedeon was accused of trivializing the Holocaust in several of his publications. The two caucuses reunited in October.

Trafficking in Persons

See the Department of State's *Trafficking in Persons Report* at www.state.gov/j/tip/rls/tiprpt/.

Persons with Disabilities

The law prohibits discrimination against persons with physical or mental disabilities in employment, education, access to health care, the judicial system, and the provision of other federal government services, including access to air travel and other transportation. The law makes no specific mention of the rights of persons with sensory or intellectual disabilities, but their rights are considered included under the other headings. NGOs disagreed on the effectiveness of government enforcement of antidiscrimination laws, and the government expressed interest in learning ways to improve its effectiveness.

Persons with disabilities faced particular difficulties finding housing. The country's approximately 500,000 children with disabilities attended school. Some persons with disabilities attended special schools, which officials contended were often better equipped to take care of such students. Some observers asserted that these institutions prevented the full integration of children with disabilities into the professional world and society as a whole.

On July 19, an amendment to the federal Act on Equal Opportunities for Persons with Disabilities mandates that federal buildings and the webpages of federal authorities be gradually made more accessible to persons with disabilities; establishes an arbitration body with the federal Commissioner for Matters relating to Disabled Persons; and provides financial support for disability associations from the Federal Ministry of Labor and Social Affairs. Disability NGOs criticized that the new law because its accessibility demands cover only federal buildings and do not extend to local job centers, youth welfare offices, and private buildings.

Progress in improving access to public buildings and transportation and integrating students with disabilities into regular schools varied from region to region. Access for persons with disabilities to public transportation in rural areas was limited.

National/Racial/Ethnic Minorities

Harassment of foreigners and members of racial minorities remained a problem throughout the country. Hostility focused on the increasing number of asylum seekers, refugees, and migrants from the Middle East and Africa.

The annual FOPC report for 2015 described 918 of the 1,485 violent "politically motivated crimes" with "right-wing extremist backgrounds" as xenophobic.

PEGIDA declined in strength. On average, only approximately 2000 demonstrators attended PEGIDA rallies in Dresden during the first half year of the year. This represented a significant decrease in PEGIDA support as compared with 2015.

On April 28, the Duesseldorf Local Court sentenced Melanie Dittmer, right-wing organizer of the Duesseldorf chapter of PEGIDA (Duegida), to eight months of probation for incitement, insult, and impeding the freedom of religion. Two Duegida marches in February and March 2015 interfered with a mosque's evening prayer. Dittmer was also responsible for the creation of the PEGIDA offshoots in Cologne and Bonn. Previously she worked in the NPD's youth organization in NRW and contributed to neo-Nazi publications.

Persons of foreign origin faced particular difficulties finding housing. FADA reported cases of landlords denying rental apartments to persons of non-ethnic-German origin, particularly of Turkish and African origin, saying that the neighborhood's population was majority ethnic German.

In July the Turkish Bil-School, a Gulen-affiliated institution in Stuttgart-Bad Cannstatt (Baden-Wuerttemberg), requested police protection after being threatened by individuals or groups claiming to be supporters of Turkish President Erdogan.

In May the NRW Ministry of Family Affairs, Children, Youth, and Culture announced an action plan to counter right-wing extremism by strengthening 166 mostly local programs. The plan increased the funding for anti-right-wing efforts by two million euros ($2.2 million) to 3.15 million euros ($3.47 million) annually.

In March 2015 the Federal Constitutional Court ruled that a headscarf ban for teachers at public schools is a violation of the right to freedom of religion. In August, Elisabeth Herzog-von der Heide, the mayor of Luckenwalde in the state of Brandenburg, terminated a woman's internship because she refused to remove her headscarf while working in the city hall. According to the mayor, the wearing of a headscarf in the city hall was a violation of the constitutional neutrality law.

The Berlin-based Network against Discrimination and Islamophobia reported cases of discrimination during job interviews. It reported a teacher was rejected from a position at a Berlin elementary school because of the Berlin neutrality law that prohibits public employees from wearing headscarves, and her case went to court. Her case led other women to report their cases.

Media reported in June that a public pool in Neustraubling in Bavaria banned swimmers from wearing burqinis. City councils in other cities, including Konstanz and Munich, publicly declared that burqinis were allowed.

Acts of Violence, Discrimination, and Other Abuses Based on Sexual Orientation and Gender Identity

The law prohibits discrimination based on sexual orientation and gender identity. When registering the birth of a child, parents may check a blank box for the gender of an intersex child.

There were no official statistics on mistreatment of lesbian, gay, bisexual, transgender, and intersex (LGBTI) persons; the availability of NGO reports on the incidence of such mistreatment varied widely in different parts of the country, although some quantitative data was available for cities with large populations of LGBTI persons. In 2015 there were 259 assaults in Berlin motivated by bias against LGBTI persons, according to the NGO Maneo. Insults accounted for 23 percent of the cases reported, injury for 29 percent, and coercion and threat for 22 percent.

In January the Protestant Church for the Rhine area began offering church weddings for same-sex couples living in a registered partnership.

HIV and AIDS Social Stigma

The NGO German AIDS Foundation reported that societal discrimination against persons with HIV/AIDS ranged from isolation and negative comments from acquaintances, family, and friends to bullying at work and denial of service at medical facilities (see section 7.d.). A domestic AIDS service NGO criticized authorities in Bavaria for their continued practice of mandatory HIV testing for asylum seekers.

Other Societal Violence or Discrimination

There were increasing instances of actual or attempted mob violence against asylum seekers, refugees and, migrants, and persons perceived as Muslims in some parts of the country (see section 2.d.) and against Muslims (see section 6, National/Racial/Ethnic Minorities).

In 2014 a self-declared "Sharia Police" group staged patrols in Wuppertal, NRW, to counter "non-Muslim behavior," including alcohol consumption, gambling, and smoking and to pressure youth to convert to Islam. In December 2015 the Wuppertal local court ruled that the men did not violate a ban on wearing uniforms. In May 2016 the Duesseldorf Higher Regional Court overruled this decision and allowed the prosecution of eight members of the "Sharia Police." On November 21, the local court in Wuppertal, NRW, acquitted seven of the members. Proceedings for the eighth member of the group were suspended, pending a separate trial in which he was a defendant on an unrelated terrorism charge.

On September 27, two homemade bombs exploded in Dresden at the door of a mosque and near the International Conference Center. There were no injuries. At year's end police were investigating the incidents.

Section 7. Worker Rights

a. Freedom of Association and the Right to Collective Bargaining

The constitution, federal legislation, and government regulations provide for the right of employees to form and join independent unions, bargain collectively, and conduct legal strikes. The law prohibits antiunion discrimination and offers legal remedies to claim damages, including the reinstatement of unlawfully dismissed workers. The government generally respected these rights.

No laws or regulations limit these labor rights. In addition while civil servants are free to form or join unions, their wages and working conditions are determined by legislation and not by collective bargaining. All civil servants (including some teachers, postal workers, railroad employees, and police), and members of the armed forces are prohibited from striking. All employees, whether trade union members or not, usually benefit from the provisions of the bargained collective agreement.

Employers are generally free to decide whether to be a party to a collective bargaining agreement; however, companies need to apply the provisions of a collective agreement if the Ministry of Labor and Social Affairs declares a collective bargaining agreement as generally binding. Employers not legally bound by collective bargaining agreements also often made use of them to determine part or all employment conditions of their employees. Employers may contest in court a strike's proportionality and a trade union's right to take strike actions. Legislation fails to establish clear criteria, but case law provides specific measures on strike matters.

The government enforced the applicable laws with adequate resources. Actions and measures by employers to limit or violate freedom of association and the right to collective bargaining are considered unlawful and void and lead to fines. Penalties were adequate and remediation efforts were sufficient.

The government and employers respected freedom of association and the right to collective bargaining. There were reports that a few employers--primarily owner-managed companies--interfered in the work council elections, in which employees in companies with five or more employees elect representatives to participate in discussions and cooperation with the company's management. Laws regulate cooperation between management and work councils, including the right of the workers to information about company operations that could affect them. The penalty for employers who interfere in work councils' elections and operations is up to one year in prison or a fine. Work councils are independent from labor unions but often have close ties to the sector's labor movement.

b. Prohibition of Forced or Compulsory Labor

The constitution and federal law prohibit all forms of forced or compulsory labor; nevertheless, there were reports of forced labor. Penalties for forced labor range from six months to 10 years in prison and were sufficiently stringent to deter violations.

The government effectively enforced the law when companies were discovered employing forced labor, but NGOs questioned the adequacy of resources to investigate and prosecute forced labor, and courts at times failed to impose appropriate sentences. Some traffickers received suspended sentences which limited the effectiveness of government enforcement efforts.

There were reports of forced labor involving adults, mainly in agriculture and construction. There were also reports in restaurants, hotels, meat-processing plants, seasonal industries, and domestic households. In 2015, the latest year for which statistics were available, police completed 19 labor-trafficking investigations which identified 54 victims, mostly from Bulgaria (63 percent) followed by Romania (7 percent), and Hungary (7 percent).

Also see the Department of State's *Trafficking in Persons Report* at www.state.gov/j/tip/rls/tiprpt/.

c. Prohibition of Child Labor and Minimum Age for Employment

The law prohibits the employment of children younger than 15 years of age with a few exceptions: Children aged 13 or 14 may perform farm work for up to three hours per day or perform services such as delivering newspapers, babysitting, and dog walking for up to two hours per day. Children of these ages may not work during school hours, before 8 a.m., or after 6 p.m. The type of work must not pose any risk to the security, health, or development of the child and must not prevent the child from obtaining schooling and training. Children are not allowed to work with hazardous materials, carry or handle items weighing more than 22 pounds, perform work requiring an unsuitable posture, or work that exposes them to the risk of an accident (especially by machine operation or animal care). Children between three and 14 years of age may take part in cultural performances, but there are strict limits on the kind of activity, number of hours, and time of day.

The government effectively enforced these laws. Courts may punish violators with fines of up to 15,000 euros ($16,500) and a prison sentence of up to one year for severe cases that intentionally cause serious risk to the child's health and employability. These penalties were adequate to deter violations.

Isolated cases of child labor might have occurred in small, family-owned businesses, such as cafes, restaurants, family farms, and grocery stores.

Inspections by the regional inspection agencies and the resources and remediation available to them were adequate to ensure broad compliance.

d. Discrimination with Respect to Employment and Occupation

The Equal Treatment Law, which focuses on equal treatment with respect to employment and occupation, prohibits discrimination based on ethnic origin or race (including skin color and language), age, sex, religion or belief or world view (including political opinion), sexual orientation and gender identity, disability, and HIV positive status or other communicable diseases. The law protects against discrimination in all areas of occupation and employment, from recruitment, self-employment, and promotion, to career advancement. Although social origin and citizenship are not explicitly listed as grounds of discrimination in the Equal Treatment Law, persons who fell victim of such discrimination have other means to assert legal claims.

The government effectively enforced these laws and regulations. The law obliges employers to protect employees from discrimination at work. Employees who believe they are victims of discrimination have a right to file an official complaint and to have the complaint heard. If an employer remains inactive or fails to protect the employee effectively, employees may remove themselves from places and situations of discrimination without losing employment or pay. In cases of violations of the Equal Treatment Law, victims of discrimination are entitled to injunctions, removal, and material or nonmaterial damages set by court decision. Penalties were sufficient to deter violations. According to a 2015 FADA survey, almost half of all discrimination cases took place in a work environment or during the recruitment process. The most common grounds of employment-related discrimination were age, sex, and gender identity. Persons of foreign origin and persons with disabilities faced particular difficulties finding employment.

According to a study conducted by the Hans-Boeckler Foundation, the unemployment rate among immigrants--particularly those from Turkey, former Yugoslavia, and non-European countries--was twice as high as that of the general population. Immigrants were also more likely to have temporary or marginal employment with fewer prospects for career and wage advancement, regardless of their qualification level. According to FADA, job applicants with foreign-sounding names were up to 24 percent less likely to receive a job interview than equally qualified applicants with German names. The public sector sometimes conducted similar studies using anonymized applications, but it was not yet a widespread practice.

A 2015 study by the German Statistics Office found that women's wages were on average 21 percent less than those of men, and women less frequently held managerial and executive positions. The gap was considerably larger in the western part of the country (23 percent) than in the east (8 percent). The survey also found that the gender pay gap increased with age. Based on 2010 data, the latest to include structural adjustments, the gap narrowed to 7 percent when adjusted for structural differences (such as profession or sector, education, part-time and full-time employment). FADA reported that women were at a disadvantage regarding promotions, often due to interruptions for child rearing.

In 2015 women occupied 6 percent of the positions on management boards and 20 percent of positions on supervisory boards in the country's top 200 companies. The law imposes a gender quota of 30 percent for supervisory boards of certain publicly traded corporations. The law also requires approximately 3,500 companies to set and publish self-determined targets for increasing the share of women in leading positions (executive boards and management) by 2017 and to report on their performance.

In July the NRW state parliament passed a law that removes structural disadvantages faced by women in civil service. The law gives women with essentially equal qualifications for leadership positions preferential treatment over men until a 50-percent quota is reached for the specific hierarchical level. The law was strongly debated and might face court challenges. On September 5, the Duesseldorf administrational court ruled this passage of the service law unconstitutional. A police officer took legal action against the promotion of several female police officers. This judgment was the first in an expected wave of lawsuits. The judges argued that such provisions are not within the state jurisdiction and according to the federal law promotions were strictly by skills and not by sex. On September 12, Minister President Hannelore Kraft announced that the NRW government would appeal the verdict.

There were also reports of employment discrimination against persons with disabilities. The unemployment rate among persons with disabilities was 13.9 percent in 2015, considerably higher than that of the general population. The government undertook a number of measures to promote the employment of persons with disabilities. Employers with 20 or more employees must hire persons with more significant disabilities to fill at least 5 percent of all positions. There are special provisions for companies with 20-40 employees (one position for persons with disabilities) and 40-60 (two positions for persons with disabilities).

Companies that fail to meet these quotas face a monthly fine of 105-260 euros ($116-$286) for each required position not filled by a person with disabilities.

In May the Federal Constitutional Court ruled in favor of two teachers who sued NRW because the state denied them permanent civil servant status due to age. The court ruled the age limit to be unjustified and a massive infringement of the fundamental right of freedom to pursue a professional activity.

In 2015 the NRW government raised the age limit to enter permanent civil service status from 40 to 42 years old. In other states the age limits are 45 years (Bavaria), 47 years (Thuringia), or 50 years (Hesse). In response, the Protective Association of Employed Teachers filed a complaint with the EU Commission in Brussels for violation of the ban on age discrimination. The proceedings are expected to take approximately one year.

The law provides for equal treatment of foreign workers, although foreign workers faced some wage discrimination. For example, employers, particularly in the construction sector, sometimes paid lower wages to seasonal workers from Eastern Europe who were in the country on temporary work permits. According to a 2013 study by the Institute of Labor Market Research, the wage gap between foreign workers and other workers narrowed as the foreign workers' stay in the country lengthened; nevertheless, information from 2008 indicated that, after eight years working in the country, foreign workers earned 28 percent less than the average worker.

e. Acceptable Conditions of Work

In January 2015 the country's first statutory countrywide minimum wage of 8.50 euros ($9.35) per hour (before tax) entered into effect. The law exempts young persons under 18 and the long-term unemployed during their first six months in a new job. The remaining four sectors with existing collective agreements that include minimum wages below the statutory minimum wage level have until January 2017 to transition. Sectors that set their own minimum wages include electrical trades, painting, scaffolding, roofing, waste management, large-scale laundries, cleaning services, nursing care, hairdressing, meat processing, special mining services, and temporary employment agencies. Sector-wide minimum wages, which were generally lower in the eastern parts of the country than in the west, ranged from 7.90 euros ($8.69) per hour in agriculture and forestry (in the East) to 15.73 euros ($17.30) per hour in the money processing and valuables transportation industries in the western state of NRW. The national statutory minimum wage of 8.50 euros ($9.35) per hour is 48 percent of the median hourly wage for full-time employees in the country, putting it below the internationally defined "low-wage" level of two-thirds of the national median wage. According to the EU Statistical Office, in 2015 persons living in a single household in the country with an income of less than 12,396 euros ($13,636) per year (60 percent of the national median income) were at risk of poverty. More than 13 million persons (16.7 percent of the population) fell below this threshold.

Federal regulations set the standard workday at eight hours, with a maximum of 10 hours, and limit the average workweek to 48 hours. Collective bargaining agreements, which directly or indirectly affect 79 percent of the working population, regulate the number of weekly working hours and the average maximum workweek under current agreements is 37.7 hours. According to the Federal Statistical Office, the average workweek of full-time employees was 41.5 hours in 2015. The law requires a break after no more than six hours of work, stipulates regular breaks totaling at least 30 minutes, and sets a minimum of 24 days of paid annual leave in addition to official holidays. Provisions for overtime, holiday, and weekend pay varied, depending upon the applicable collective bargaining agreement. Such agreements or individual contracts prohibited excessive compulsory overtime and protected workers against arbitrary employer requests.

The Customs Office's Financial Control Illicit Work Unit (FKS) is responsible for monitoring compliance with the statutory and sector-wide minimum wages and hours of work. The FKS conducted checks on 43,000 companies and 360,000 individuals in 2015 and completed 104,000 criminal proceedings. Employees may sue companies if employers fail to comply with the Minimum Wage Act. Courts may sentence employers who violate the provisions to pay a fine of up to 500,000 euros ($550,000).

An extensive set of laws and regulations govern occupational safety and health. A comprehensive system of worker insurance carriers enforced safety requirements in the workplace. Workers may remove themselves from situations that endanger their health or safety without jeopardizing their employment, and authorities effectively protected employees in this situation.

The Federal Ministry of Labor and Social Affairs and its counterparts in the states effectively monitored and enforced occupational safety and health standards through a network of government bodies, including the Federal Agency for Occupational Safety and Health. At the local level, professional and trade associations--self-governing public corporations with delegates representing both employers and unions--as well as work councils oversaw worker safety.

The number of inspectors declined in recent years, but there were enough to ensure compliance. In 2014, 2,538 inspectors visited approximately 286,000 companies to examine working conditions and compliance with occupational safety and health regulations. In 2014 there were 409,702 complaints. Employees may sue employers who do not comply with occupational safety and health regulations. In cases in which the employer culpably infringed the duty to have regard for the welfare of its employees, a court may sentence the company to pay compensation to the affected employees and a fine of up to 25,000 euros ($27,500). In severe cases offenders the law provides for prison sentences of up to one year. These penalties were adequate.

During 2015 the number of reported work accidents decreased to approximately 866,000 incidents despite growing employment numbers. There were fewer than 22 accidents in the workplace for every 1,000 full-time workers--the lowest level since reunification of the country. Most accidents occurred in the construction, wood and metalworking, and transportation industries. The number of workplace fatalities also decreased to 470.